DISGUSTING & DREADFUL SCIENCE

Smelly Farts

and other body horrors

by Anna Claybourne

W

FRANKLIN WATTS

LONDON•SYDNEY

First published in 2014 by Franklin Watts

Copyright © Franklin Watts 2014

Franklin Watts
338 Euston Road
London NW1 3BH

Franklin Watts Australia
Level 17/207 Kent Street, Sydney, NSW 2000

Produced by Penny Worms & Graham Rich, Book Packagers

A CIP catalogue record for this book is available from the British Library.

Dewey Decimal Classification Number: 612

ISBN 978 1 4451 3563 2
Library eBook ISBN 978 1 4451 3564 9

Printed in China

Franklin Watts is a division of Hachette Children's Books, an Hachette UK company.

www.hachette.co.uk

Picture credits
Alamy: 13c (SCPhotos). **Corbis images:** 19c (John Spellman/Retna Ltd). **Dreamstime:** 8b (Guniita), 17t (oxygen64).
iStockphoto.com: title page (Dean Murray), eyeball cartoon (Elaine Barker), cover (man/Suzanne Tucker), 11br
(Maica), 19b (sdominick). **Science Photo Library:** 24b (Steve Gschmeissner). **Shutterstock.com:** angry monster
cartoon (Yayayoyo), cover (skeleton/Jesse Christoffersen) (girl/PathDoc) (toilet roll/Natalia Dobryanskaya) (feet/
Artieskg), cover and 5cl (boy/WEExp), 4br (PathDoc), 5tr (Jesse Christoffersen), 5b (PathDoc), 6t (Kuttelvaserova
Stuchelova), 6cl (Giovanni Cancemi), 6b (blambca), 7c (paulvg), 7br (Jon Larter), 7bl (blambca), 9t (NikolayN), 9b
(Vlue), 10b (Nikita Chisnikov), 11tl (pdesign), 11tr (Crepesoles), 11bl (Shevs), 12t (Vlue), 12br (Yoko Design), 12bl
(Aleksandar Todorovic), 13b (deepspacedave), 14t (HitToon.com), 14c (amudsen), 14b (fusebulb), 15cr (DenisNata),
15tr (Michael William), 15bl (raysay), 16t (Sukpaiboonwat), 16br (Sebastian Kaulitzki), 16bl (ronstik), 17c (chaika), 17b
(oksana2010), 18tr (Don Purcell), 18cr (Julien Tromeur), 18b (kzww), 19t (GRei), 20cl (schankz), 20br (filmfoto), 20br
cartoons (blambca), 21t (Javier Brosch), 21c (blambca), 21br (Johan Larsen), 22c (decade3d), 22b (Simone van den
Berg), 23t (Adisa), 23 bubbles (romrf), 23b (Ana Blazic Pavlovic), 24t (Lyudmyla Kharlamova), 25t (Juan Gaertner),
25b (falk), 25cl (Miramiska), 25cr (novkota1), 26b (Alta Oosthuizen), 27t (Geo-grafika), 27b (sydeen), 28r (Jacek
Chabraszewski), 28l (Ekarin Apirakthanakorn), 29t (slaystorm), 29cl (John Larter), 29b (NinaMalyna). **wikimedia:** 15br.
wikipedia: 27c (Hieronymus Bosch).

All other illustrations by Graham Rich

Every attempt has been made to clear copyright. Should there be any inadvertent omission,
please apply to the publisher for rectification.

Contents

Your amazing, gross body!

Your body is an amazing thing. It has millions of moving parts and can do hundreds of different jobs – and, of course, you depend on it to keep you alive. Yet there are quite a few body bits, functions and substances that we find rude, even disgusting. Think of farts, poo, wee and slimy snot! How would you feel about a handful of toenail trimmings or earwax? Ugh! And blood can scare some people so much, they faint!

Ouch!

One of the things we find most horrifying is when the body goes wrong. People are grossed out by scabs, rotten teeth, pus seeping out of a wound, or a big bursting boil - because these things could be a sign of a harmful infection (an invasion of germs).

BUURRRP!

Ooops!

Bless you!

In polite company we put our hands over our mouths when we burp, sneeze or cough, and say "Excuse me!" to make it okay.

Excuse me!

Look inside

You're not meant to be able to see inside your body – if you can, it means something horrible has happened, such as a bad injury! So we're often revolted by the sight of human insides, and don't like thinking about things like eyeballs and brains.

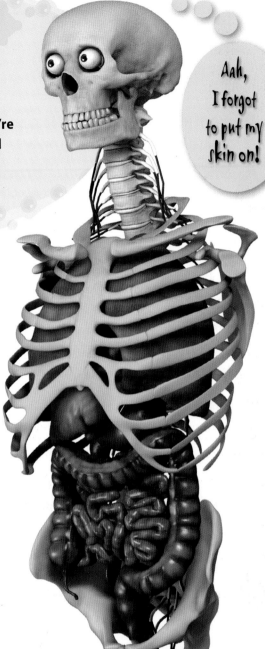

Aah, I forgot to put my skin on!

Stop that!

Most people learn from a young age that some body activities, like picking your nose, are not very polite or hygienic!

Bleuuurrrgggh!

One of the most disgusting things of all is vomit, because we link it with illness and germs. (Even though you could easily throw up for other reasons, like feeling dizzy or seasick!)

DID YOU KNOW?

Your body is home to billions of tiny living things called bacteria. What are they doing there? Read on to find out...

5

Sticky snot

I t's runny. It's sticky. It can be embarrassing! So what is snot? Snot is simply mucus produced in your nose. It's really important stuff because it is a brilliant germ-catcher – it waits inside your nose to trap and catch germs in the air as you breathe in. The reason snot is so sticky is to help germs get stuck in it.

Germ-killer

Snot also contains germ-killing chemicals, to help kill the bugs before they can make you ill. Thanks to snot, you don't get anywhere near as many coughs and colds as you could, because it keeps germs out of your lungs. But when you do get a cold, your body goes into overdrive making loads of snot!

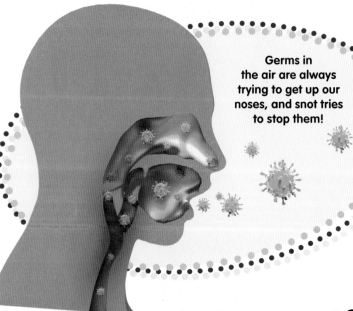

Germs in the air are always trying to get up our noses, and snot tries to stop them!

Eeehhh-CHOO!

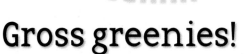

Gross greenies!

Snot is normally quite pale or clear, but when you have a cold it can look green. This is because your body sends germ-killing blood cells to your nose and lungs to help fight the germs, and they have a whitish-green colour.

6

See for Yourself

Make fake snot

To make fake snot, mix a teaspoon of runny honey with half a teaspoon of cornflour and a tiny drop of green food colouring. Smear your "snot" onto a plate. Then use small seeds, such as poppy seeds or sesame seeds, as germs. Flick them at the snot to see how they get stuck!

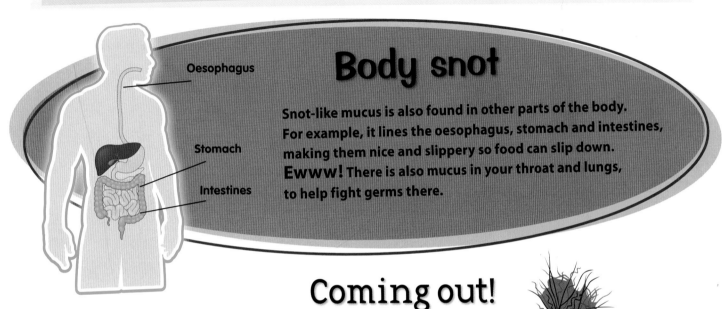

Oesophagus

Stomach

Intestines

Body snot

Snot-like mucus is also found in other parts of the body. For example, it lines the oesophagus, stomach and intestines, making them nice and slippery so food can slip down. **Ewww!** There is also mucus in your throat and lungs, to help fight germs there.

Coming out!

Bogeys, or boogers, are dried-up, solid bits of snot that fall out of your nose (or get picked out). This dried snot usually ends up crumbling away and turning into household dust – along with other disgusting dust ingredients, such as skin flakes, hairs and dandruff.

Yuck!

When you sneeze, droplets of snot can zoom out of your nose at 80 km/h.

skin and scabs

Skin is a very important body part. It covers you all over, keeping body bits together, protecting them from germs, and helping to keep you both warm and cool. But when something goes wrong with your skin, it's easy to see – making you go "Ugh! What's THAT?"

Yuck!

In 2003, a tourist who was lost in the Colombian rainforest for 12 days staved off his hunger pangs by eating a large scab he picked off his face!

Scabby!

A big, crispy scab may not be nice to look at, but scabs are very useful. Your body makes them to fill in and cover over cuts and scrapes, keeping out germs while the skin underneath heals. You should NOT pick them – let them fall off in their own time!

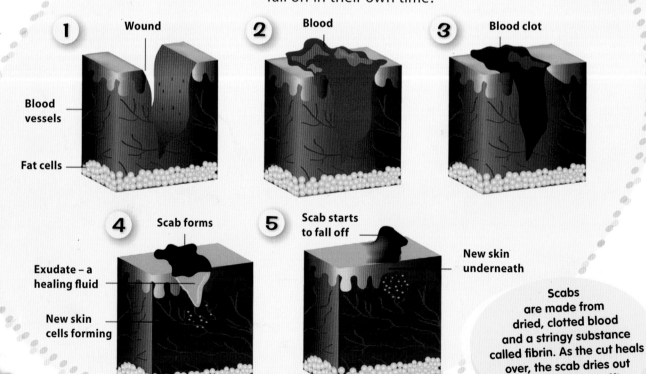

1. Wound — Blood vessels — Fat cells

2. Blood

3. Blood clot

4. Scab forms — Exudate – a healing fluid — New skin cells forming

5. Scab starts to fall off — New skin underneath

Scabs are made from dried, clotted blood and a stringy substance called fibrin. As the cut heals over, the scab dries out and then drops off!

Oozing with pus

Pus is the whitish-yellow gloopy stuff you can sometimes see coming out of a sore, cut or zit. Most people find it disgusting, and this is because we know it's a sign of infection. When germs get into your skin, white blood cells arrive to fight them. Many of the white blood cells die, and combined with the germs, they make the creamy-coloured pus.

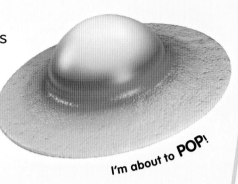

I'm about to **POP!**

Zit alert

Zits or spots happen when pores (tiny holes in your skin) get blocked with oil or dirt, and bacteria (a type of germ) build up inside the hair follicles below. This makes a bump on the skin, which some people squeeze and pop! It's also possible to get a much bigger, deeper version of a zit, called a boil. People sometimes have to go to hospital to have a boil cut open and cleaned out. Erk!

Some zits really hurt! That's because the pores become swollen and the swelling causes pain. OUCH!

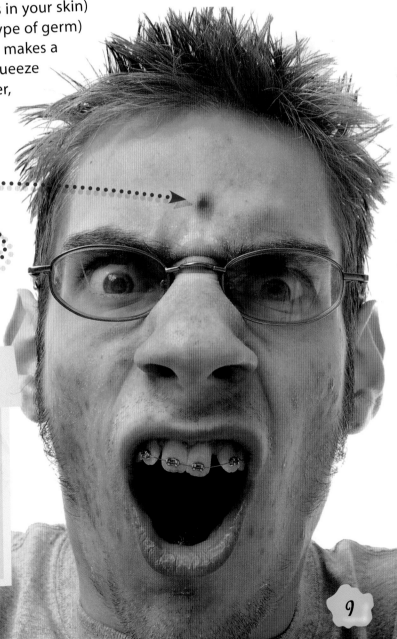

See for Yourself

Skin scan

Have a good close look at the skin on your arm through a magnifying glass. You'll see the tiny hairs all over it, and the rough, scaly surface. Every day, millions of skin cells flake off our skin and turn into dust!

9

stinky sweat

If you've been playing football or dancing until you're sweaty, or sweltering on a hot sunny day, you might feel a bit drenched and clammy. So why do we leak liquid out of our skin? It seems like a strangely disgusting thing to do!

Yuck!

Sweat is almost all water, but it also contains traces of salt, sugar, ammonia and urea. Ammonia and urea are chemicals produced when your digestive system breaks down food.

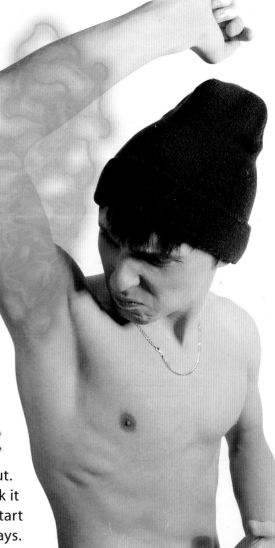

Cool!

The reason you sweat is that it's a brilliant way to cool you down. Your skin contains over two million sweat glands – tiny organs that release the sweat. Each one leads to a tiny hole, or sweat pore, in your skin, where the sweat can escape. As it flows onto the surface of your skin, it starts to evaporate, or turn into a gas, and float off into the air. This uses up heat energy from your body – and you cool down.

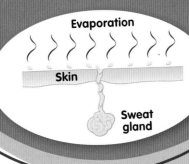

Evaporation

Skin

Sweat gland

Sweet sweat

Sweat isn't actually very smelly when it first comes out. But after a while, bacteria on the skin start to break it down into stinky chemicals. That's why we can start to smell a bit if we don't wash for a few days.

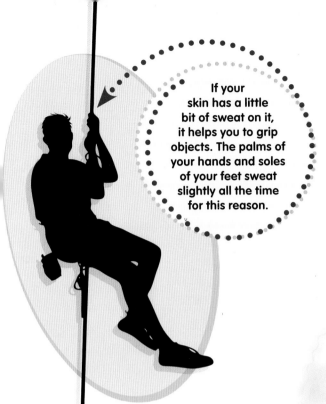

If your skin has a little bit of sweat on it, it helps you to grip objects. The palms of your hands and soles of your feet sweat slightly all the time for this reason.

See for Yourself

Sweat test

To see how sweat works, collect some warm water in a bowl and dab some onto one of your hands using a tissue. Now blow hard on each of your hands in turn. The damp hand should feel cooler as the water evaporates – even though the water itself was not cold.

PHHEEEWW!!!

Sweaty feet

The feet are the sweatiest parts of the body, with 500,000 sweat glands between them. A man's feet can produce two whole cupfuls of sweat in a day! As they're usually bundled up in socks and shoes the sweat can't escape, leading to cheesy-smelling feet.

DID YOU KNOW?

Dogs don't sweat like humans do. Instead, if they get hot or stressed, they pant to cool themselves down. Water evaporating from their mouths has the same cooling effect as sweat evaporating from our bodies. Horses, however, are like us. Sometimes, you can see white, frothy sweat on an excited racehorse before a race.

Horrible hair and nasty nails

People spend lots of time and money making their hair and nails look lovely – but once they've been snipped off – YUCK! A clump of hair down the plughole or a pile of toenails left on the sofa could turn your stomach.

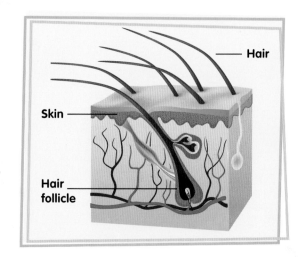

Hairy bodies

What is hair? It's actually very similar to skin, and is made inside the skin from a type of skin cell. Each hair grows from a special cup-shaped hair follicle, where the hair is built and pushed up through the skin. An average human has five million of these hair follicles. They are found all over your body, except for on the palms of your hands, the soles of your feet, your eyelids and your lips.

People are far less hairy than many animals. We only have a few areas of thick hair, such as on our heads, and for men, on their chins! Animals, such as monkeys and rabbits, use their hair (or fur) to keep warm.

Hair

Skin

Hair follicle

See for Yourself

Nail speed

Choose one of your fingernails or toenails and don't trim it for a month. Measure it at the start and end of your experiment. How much did it grow? Can you work out how much it would grow in a year?

Human claws

Fingernails and toenails are the human equivalent of animal claws. Like hair, they are made of keratin, a tough substance that grows from the skin. Also like hair, they keep growing longer and longer. Once they grow away from the skin, hair and nails are dead. Maybe that's why we don't like to see the trimmings lying around. No one wants to look at fallen-off dead body bits!

Some people grow their nails as long as they possibly can instead of trimming them. The longest nails ever recorded were over 8 metres!

Ouch!

Nails, especially toenails, can be infected by some types of fungus (in the same kingdom as mushrooms and mould). The fungus can make the nail turn yellow and crumbly - and if it's really bad, the whole nail drops off! Ewww!

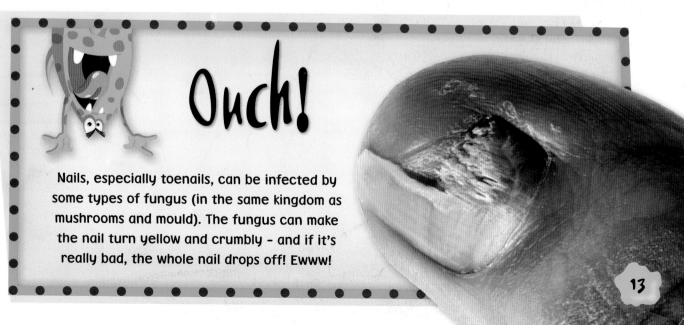

13

Farts, poo and wee

Whoooops!

Which are the most disgusting and dreadful, gross and revolting body bits of all? It has to be the smelly, horrible waste products our bodies get rid of every day. If they stayed inside us, they'd make us ill – so they've got to come out!

Eww! Poo!

Why is poo disgusting? It's made of all the bits of food we don't need – things like sweetcorn skins and vegetable seeds – that have spent several days being mushed up with stomach acid, then squeezed through your intestines. To make matters worse, this leftover mush is mixed with a large helping of the bacteria that live in your intestines, and a greenish, sticky substance called bile that helps your body digest fat. These things combined result in poo's brown colour.

Stinky!

The smell of poo is really revolting. But why? The bacteria it contains don't do any harm when they are in your intestines. But if they get in your mouth, the germs can make you very ill. We naturally find poo horrifying and stinky because this makes us stay away from it – protecting us from the danger.

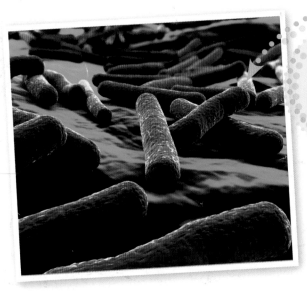

Just a few of the billions of bacteria that live in our intestines.

You have more gut bacteria living in you than you have actual body cells of your own!

It was him!

Was that you?!

The intestine bacteria actually help us to digest our food. They feed on it and break it down into useful chemicals for our bodies. But as this happens, they also create their own waste product – gas. This gas occasionally escapes out of your bottom, laced with pooey smells, in the form of a fart. PARP!

What is wee?

Wee is a different waste product. It's made by two organs, called the kidneys, as they filter your blood and remove waste chemicals and water. The wee, or urine, is stored in your bladder, which is like a stretchy bag, until you go to the toilet. And wee is not actually that disgusting. Before it leaves your body, it is sterile, meaning it contains no germs. After a while, though, it does become very smelly!

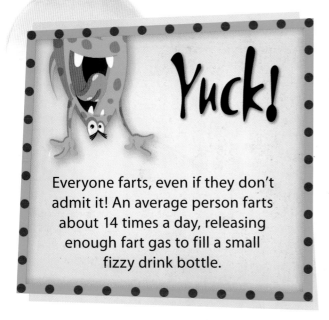

Yuck!

Everyone farts, even if they don't admit it! An average person farts about 14 times a day, releasing enough fart gas to fill a small fizzy drink bottle.

Le Pétomane was a star of the stage in the 1890s. His act showcased his amazing farting ability, including blowing out candles!

15

Blood and gore

Blood is absolutely essential for human life. Our hearts constantly pump our blood around our bodies, through an incredibly complex network of blood vessels, carrying oxygen, food, water and waste to and from all our cells. We depend on it every second of every day. So why are some people terrified of it?

Aaarrggh! Blood!

If you can see blood, that usually means there's been an injury. The heart keeps pumping the blood, and it flows quickly out of the cut or wound. And that means it's time to panic! As humans, we know that losing blood is a bad thing. Panicking makes us react quickly to stop the blood flow, with a bandage or by grabbing and squeezing the injured body part.

Blood vessels
Heart

In some people, the panic provoked by blood goes a bit too far. They only have to see a tiny speck of blood and they collapse or scream! Many people also hate seeing their blood being taken with a needle for a blood test.

The horror

Yuck!

As blood is a liquid it can spread out very thinly. People often think someone has lost a lot of blood when in fact it's only a small amount.

Strangely, though, many people enjoy scaring themselves by watching films or reading stories about gross, gruesome and gory events. Blood-soaked horror stories and movies are among the most popular of all!

Putting blood back

In some accidents, people do lose quite a bit of blood. You can lose around 10 per cent of your blood without a problem – the body will replace it. But losing a lot is dangerous. If someone loses too much, they can have a blood transfusion – an injection of carefully checked and screened blood donated by someone else.

Blue blood

Aarrgghh!

Why is blood red? It's because iron is an important ingredient in our blood. Iron mixed with oxygen gives blood its red colour. But some animals, like octopuses and horseshoe crabs, have copper in their blood instead, making theirs blue!

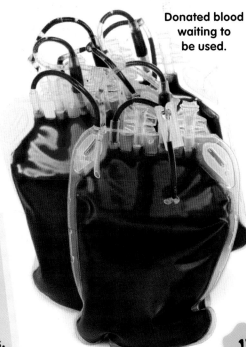

Donated blood waiting to be used.

See for Yourself

How much blood?

The average human has about 5 litres of blood. To see what this looks like, fill a bucket with 5 litres of water. Now take it outside and pour it onto the ground to see how far it spreads.

Eyes and ears

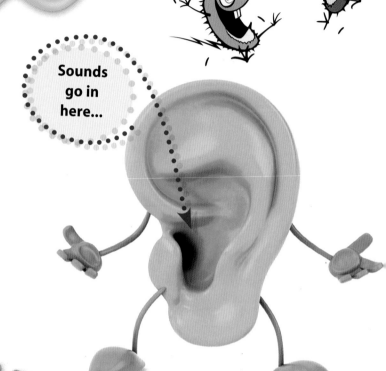

Eyes and ears are sense organs that let useful information into the body. Eyes have a hole at the front, the pupil, that lets in light so you can see. Ears have a tube leading to the delicate eardrum, which senses sound vibrations. But this means that eyes and ears are actually holes in your head where stuff can get in. That's why they come armed with their own special gunk to fight off germs.

Sounds go in here...

Earwax

Your ear wants sounds to get in, but not dangerous germs. So it makes a steady trickle of sticky, germ-zapping earwax that can trap and kill germs. The wax gradually moves out of the ear, helped by tiny movements your ear makes when you chew and speak. Clever!

However, earwax can sometimes get stuck and build up in a big lump, making it hard to hear. A doctor or nurse can "syringe" it out by squirting water into your ear. The wax sloshes out and hits the collecting bowl with a **"ping"**!

Eyeballs

Eyes are often described as beautiful, but an eyeball is not! Each of your eyes is actually a round, white ball, rolling around in its socket – a big round hole in your skull. Luckily, eyeballs can't fall out as they are held in place by muscly strings. They also have a nerve at the back that carries information to the brain about the light patterns you can see. Inside, the eyeball is filled with a thick, see-through jelly, called vitreous humour.

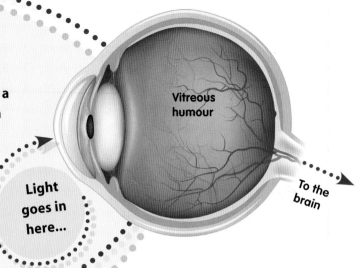

Vitreous humour

To the brain

Light goes in here...

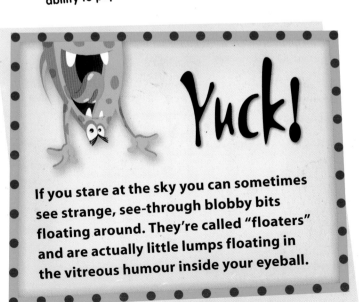

Some people have the extraordinary ability to pop out their eyes like this!

Eye snot!

Have you ever woken up in the morning and picked a bit of sandy stuff out of your eye? This is known as sleep, sleeping sand, eye sand, eye bogeys or eye boogers! – but scientists call it rheum. Your eye releases a snotty liquid containing trapped dead cells, dust and sometimes old, dead germs. In the daytime, tears wash it away, but at night it collects and dries in the corners of your eyes. If you have an eye disease, like conjunctivitis, there can be so much rheum your eyes get glued shut!

Yuck!

If you stare at the sky you can sometimes see strange, see-through blobby bits floating around. They're called "floaters" and are actually little lumps floating in the vitreous humour inside your eyeball.

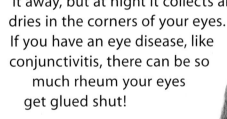

19

Teeth, spit and slobber

I could not believe my eye!

Antonie van Leeuwenhoek

When Antonie van Leeuwenhoek invented a simple microscope in the 1650s, he had a good look at some plaque from his teeth. He was amazed to discover that it was full of tiny living things, all crawling and wriggling about! Disgusting! He had discovered tooth bacteria, which live on our teeth. But what are they doing there?

Free food!

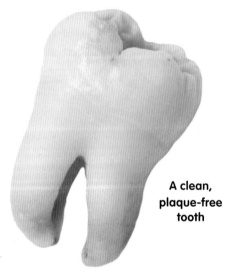

A clean, plaque-free tooth

As we use our teeth for eating, they're often covered in leftover food. That means they provide a free feast for some types of bacteria. If they're not stopped, tooth bacteria can grow and form plaque, a kind of filmy layer, on our teeth. The bacteria themselves don't harm you, but as they feed, they make waste chemicals that damage teeth. They dissolve the strong enamel covering, and the tooth can start to rot or decay inside.

What's for dinner?

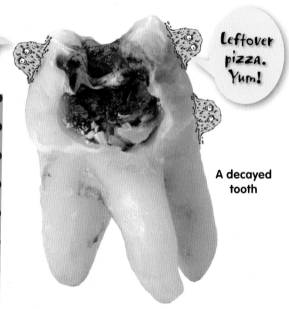

Leftover pizza. Yum!

A decayed tooth

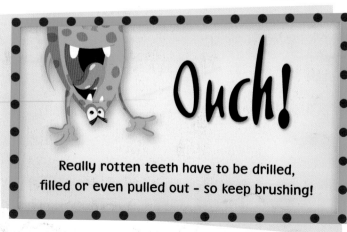

Ouch!

Really rotten teeth have to be drilled, filled or even pulled out - so keep brushing!

20

Smile!

Brushing your teeth with toothpaste cleans away the germs, protecting your teeth from decay. A big smile full of white, strong teeth is a sign that you are healthy, so humans are drawn to this, and find rotten, dirty teeth revolting to look at.

Slobbery saliva

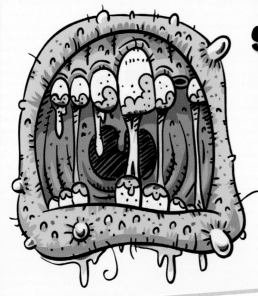

Even more disgusting is spit, or saliva. Spit is a natural, healthy part of our mouths. It helps us to chew food, and softens it to make it easier to swallow. However, spit can also contain tooth bacteria and other germs we may be carrying. That's why if we spit our saliva out, other people are shocked and horrified! In fact, spitting at people is one of the rudest, most shocking forms of behaviour there is.

Experiments have shown that people are reluctant to drink a drink they have spat in themselves. Even though we swallow our own spit all the time! Would you do it?

Gross!

See for Yourself

Saliva and taste

Dry your tongue with kitchen paper, then try eating a biscuit or crisp. It's much harder to taste without saliva, which dissolves the food and washes it over your tongue.

Sickening stomach

As you may have noticed, some very strange and disgusting sounds come from your stomach. Rumbling, growling, squirting and squelching – a lot is going on in there! Your stomach is actually a big, strong, stretchy bag for holding all the food you eat. But it doesn't just store it. It also squeezes, squashes, churns and rolls the food around to help to break it down into mush. The stomach also contains a very strong acid that mixes with the food and helps to dissolve it.

SQUIRRRT!

The squirting sounds you can sometimes hear happen as the stomach squirts the mushed-up food through a small hole, called a sphincter, at its bottom end. This leads to the intestines, where the food is gradually digested and soaked up into the body.

Stomach acid dissolving food

Sphincter

Intestines

Bleeurgh!

If we eat something poisonous, or eat too much, the stomach may decide to get rid of it by SQUEEZING hard and forcing it all back out. Vomit smells so horrible (and stings) because of the stomach acid it contains.

See for Yourself

Rumbling tummy

Put your ear to someone else's stomach after he or she has eaten to hear a selection of stomach sounds!

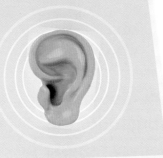

Fizzy drinks can cause terrible burps!

Burp!

Burps, or belches, happen when air or gas gets into your stomach – maybe when you're eating too fast, or if you swallow a fizzy drink containing gas bubbles. The gas rumbles back up to your throat and comes out with a strange sound.
"Pardon me!"

Acid stomach

Why doesn't the strong acid in the stomach dissolve the stomach itself? Good question! To stop this happening, the stomach is lined with a thick layer of very sticky, snot-like mucus. This means the acid can't touch the actual inside of the stomach.

BURP!

That's my boy!

Babies burp a lot as they accidentally swallow air while drinking their milk.

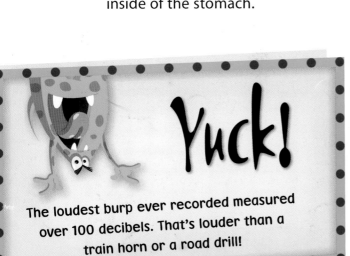

Yuck!

The loudest burp ever recorded measured over 100 decibels. That's louder than a train horn or a road drill!

Body dwellers

Your body isn't just yours. It's also a lovely, comfy home for a host of bacteria and other living things! Luckily, they tend to be too small to see, and most of them don't cause a problem – though a few are the stuff of nightmares!

Skin bacteria

Even when you've just had a wash, your skin is covered in bacteria. An average person has billions of skin bacteria, and there are up to 1,000 different types, or species. Most of them are harmless, and some can help you – for example by fighting off other, more dangerous germs. However, some can cause problems if they get into a cut, for example.

Eyelash mites

Yes, there are tiny weeny creepy-crawlies that like to live around your eyelashes. Before you panic and start trying to spot them – don't worry! They are really small, and like skin bacteria, very normal. You're not born with them, but as you get older, you have more and more chances of picking them up from other people. So most people have them by the time they're old.

There they are!
(They are coloured red in this special photograph.)

24

Gut dweller

This terrifying, alien-like monster is a tapeworm. They can get inside your body in infected food, and live in your intestines, growing longer and longer! To avoid them, don't eat raw meat, and always wash your hands before meals.

Head lice

A head louse

Head lice are tiny creatures that like to live on your head among your hair, and suck blood from your scalp. Their eggs are called nits. They are easy to spot because they are whitish, and the lice glue them to the hair strands.

Some creatures don't come to stay, but just stop by for a visit – usually to feed on your blood! Mosquitoes, midges and ticks all do this, then leave when they are full up. As they bite into you, they can sometimes pass on germs too.

Yuck!

There are many other types of lice, which are a type of wingless insect. In the past, when people washed their clothes less often, and lived in more crowded conditions, lice were much more common. They would hide in the seams of clothing and crawl about from one person to another.

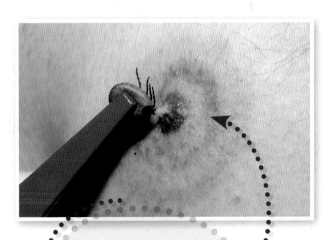

A tick latches onto your skin by digging in with its mouthparts
Ewwww!

Disgusting medicine

Medicine makes a huge difference to all of us. It can make your headache feel better when you have flu, or save your life if you have a serious disease. However, it often involves some pretty scary and disgusting scenarios – like cutting out organs, stitching up wounds, or even filling a bandage up with maggots! Yuck!

 See for Yourself

Test your reflexes

Doctors test your reflexes to see if your nervous system is working properly. One test involves tapping your knee just below the kneecap. If the reflex is working, your leg will kick suddenly. Try it!

Operations

Having an operation, or surgery, means doctors will cut your body open to fix something inside. That could mean patching up a broken bone, removing a sore appendix, digging out a massive boil, or even poking around in your brain! Luckily, these days you will get a good anaesthetic first – a special medicine that makes you fall asleep and not feel anything.

 Now, where does this go?

Even doctors and nurses sometimes faint at the sight of an operation, especially when they are training. It's normal to find it shocking to see someone's insides, even if you know it's for a good reason!

Transplant operations involve removing a diseased or failing body part, and putting in a new artificial or donated one.

Stitches

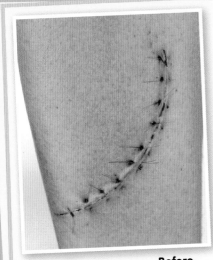

Before

To close up the skin after surgery, or to help a big cut to heal, doctors may actually have to SEW your skin together. Hopefully you'll get a good painkiller first! Sometimes the stitches have to be pulled out later – oww! Others are made of special thread that dissolves over time.

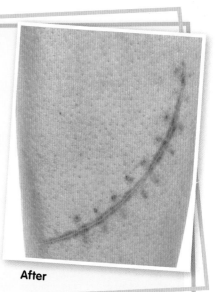

After

Traditional treatments

Old skeletons show that, long ago, people sometimes used to have neat holes cut in their skulls. This is called trepanning, and it was thought to help with mental illness, fits and even headaches. Another historical treatment was bloodletting – simply cutting you open to let some blood squirt out. This was thought to cure all kinds of illnesses!

Relax. You'll feel better soon...

Are you sure?

Creepy-crawly cures

Did you know you can have an illness or injury treated with real-live creepy-crawlies? Leeches live by sucking blood, and are sometimes used to suck blood to the skin surface to help with healing.

Yuck!

If a wound has gangrene, meaning the flesh is dying and rotting, maggots can help! They nibble away the dead flesh, leaving only the healthy bits.

27

It's the only one you've got!

Your brilliant body may have to do a few gross things, but they all happen for good reasons!

After reading this book, you might think your body is even grosser than ever. But it's still amazing! All those strange sounds, stinky smells and bits of body gunk are there for really good reasons. They actually help you survive, keep you clean and do all kinds of other useful jobs.

EARWAX, SNOT, RHEUM and SALIVA are not actually as disgusting as they seem. They contain chemicals that kill germs – so they are actually body heroes, keeping germs, the real enemies, at bay.

It's ok!

Imagine if your computer or bike could mend itself when it went wrong. That would be amazing, right? But our bodies do this all the time! Cuts and scratches start healing themselves straight away – you just have to keep them clean and covered up.

SCABS, SCARS, PUS and BLOOD CLOTS may not be very appealing. But they are all part of your body's brilliant ability to heal and fix itself when it gets damaged.

VOMIT, WEE and POO are the most disgusting things of all, but your body needs to get rid of them. If it didn't, you'd be very unwell. Better out than in!

Quick reactions

Being horrified at things going wrong with your body can be good for you – like when you see a bleeding, pus-filled sore or feel an itchy creepy-crawly nibbling your skin. Your revolted reaction tells you something bad is happening and you have to fix it or see the doctor – so it's very useful!

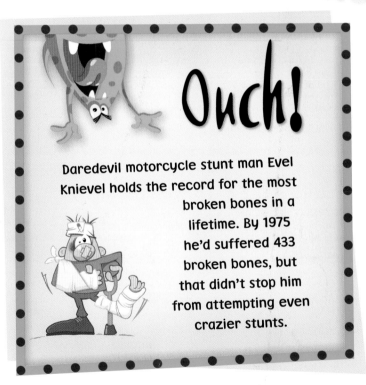

Ouch!

Daredevil motorcycle stunt man Evel Knievel holds the record for the most broken bones in a lifetime. By 1975 he'd suffered 433 broken bones, but that didn't stop him from attempting even crazier stunts.

Keep it clean

Your feelings about your body are important – even those grossed-out, disgusted ones. Finding things like poo, vomit, lice and tooth decay horrifying is a GOOD thing! It means we take care to keep ourselves clean, brush our teeth, eat sensibly and generally look after our bodies. And all that helps to keep us healthy.

Glossary

anaesthetic medicine that makes you fall asleep or not feel pain

bacteria microscopic, one-celled living things

bile the substance your body makes to help digest fatty foods

bladder stretchy bag-shaped body part where your body stores urine (wee)

blood vessels tubes that carry blood around the body

boil a large infection under the skin

cells the tiny units that living things are made up of

clot a clump of dried or hardened blood

eardrum thin layer of tightly stretched skin inside the ear

enamel the very hard, protective outer layer of teeth

evaporate to turn from a liquid into a gas

fibrin stringy substance made by the body to help form scabs

fungus a type of living thing that includes mushrooms and moulds

hair follicle small body part in the skin that a hair grows out of

infection an invasion of germs into a living thing

intestines tubes that carry food through the body

kidneys two body parts that filter the blood to remove useless substances, which the body then gets rid of in urine (wee)

leech a worm-like animal that survives by sucking blood

louse a type of wingless insect that survives by sucking blood

maggot the larva (or baby life stage) of a fly

mucus a slimy, runny body substance, such as snot

nervous system all your nerves and how they connect to your brain

plaque thin layer formed on the teeth by bacteria

pus yellowish substance in wounds and zits, made of dead white blood cells

reflex an automatic body behaviour that is hard to control

rheum another name for eye sleep

saliva another name for spit

species a particular type of living thing

sterile completely clean and containing no germs

sweat gland tiny body part in the skin that releases sweat

sweat pore tiny hole in the skin where sweat escapes

vitreous humour thick jelly inside the eyeball

Websites and Places to visit

Arm Surgery 2
www.learn4good.com/games/simulation/
doctor-hospital-games-for-kids.htm
Interactive game that lets you be a surgeon
working on an arm operation.

Kidshealth: How the Body Works
kidshealth.org/kid/htbw/
Lots of body facts, videos and things to do.

Science Kids: Human Body
www.sciencekids.co.nz/humanbody.html
Games, quizzes, experiments, projects,
pictures and videos, all to do with the
human body.

The Royal Institution: Human Body games
rigb.org/education/games/human-body
More games, quizzes and interactive
activities about the human body.

Hunterian Museum
Royal College of Surgeons,
35-43 Lincoln's Inn Fields,
London, WC2A 3PE, UK
A museum full of surgical specimens,
and other exhibits such as a key-hole
surgery simulator.
www.rcseng.ac.uk/museums/hunterian

Science Museum
Exhibition Road,
South Kensington,
London SW7 2DD, UK
A museum full of fun and
interactive exhibits.
www.sciencemuseum.org.uk

Surgeons' Hall Museums
The Royal College of Surgeons of Edinburgh
Nicolson Street,
Edinburgh EH8 9DW, UK
Another surgical museum, focusing on
the history of surgery and the study of
diseases.
www.museum.rcsed.ac.uk

Museum of Science
1 Science Park
Boston, MA 02114, USA
A museum with fascinating permanent
exhibitions on the human body.
www.mos.org

The Health Museum
1515 Hermann Dr.
Houston, Texas 77004, USA
A museum dedicated to health, medical
science and the human body.
www.mhms.org

Index